Summer Madonnas

Lessons That Your Man Can't Teach ...

Summer Madonnas
Written by Rahfeal Gordon

RahGor Motivations & Publishing

Copyright© 2013 by Rahfeal Gordon. All rights reserved, including the right to reproduce this book or portions thereof in any form whatsoever – without the written permission of the publisher. For information contact RahGor Motivations & Publishing.

978-0-9889954-9-9

RahGor Motivations
45 Rockefeller Plaza
630 Fifth Avenue, 20th Floor
New York, NY 10111
Office: (646) 358-4966
Fax: (646) 358-4878
info@rahgor.com
www.RahGor.com

Written by Rahfeal Gordon
Edited by Rob Hasting
Cover Photo by Tinnetta Bell
Layout Design by Michael Ivery
Project Manager: Melissa Gutzmore

RahGor Publishing's books are available through most book stores and online book sellers. For bulk discounts and further information, contact our offices.

Manufactured in the United States of America

Book Dedication

To You....
The finest woman in the room.

It's Okay Baby....I Won't Let You Fall

It's Not Your Fault
What You Expect
It's Called Love
The Reflection of Your Light
Takes Time To Be Good Wine
Overdosing in Paris
Make Sure Your Stilettos Are Stable
He Chooses But You Accept
Boss Talk
Boyfriend vs. Husband
Alpha Man
Never Go Unnoticed in the World
In the Mean Time
Piano Keys
Getting the Right Advice
Lesson Learned
The True Super Woman
Tired of Being Sick and Tired

Keep Walking
The Drama Woman
Why Set Low Standards
Relationships
Yesterday
Mother 2 Be
Luggage in a New Relationship
Revolving Door
Self Esteem
Difference between Two Children
Pump Your Brakes Little Lady
Homeless Woman
No Means No
Heaven
Beating the Pink Slip
126 Pocketbook Quotes

"Summer Madonnas"

A group of **beautiful** women who are **invested** in and **admired** through words by men of great **stature.**

"Je serai poète et toi poésie." - Francois Coppee

It's Not Your Fault

So let me take this time to make a statement to the females who are reading this book. I want to take the time to apologize for all the wrong situations that men have put you through. First, let me say that it wasn't your fault. I want to apologize for all the men who are still trying to make you feel as though you aren't beautiful, gorgeous, and intelligent. I will tell you again that it isn't your fault. They say a man becomes a man when he can accept his faults, but a man becomes ideal when he accepts total responsibility for the pain that he has inflicted upon you. So, I say to you that I take full responsibility for the misguidance, disrespect, and non-healthy conversations you have experienced.

But there is something I omitted while stating that I take full responsibly for the mistakes of my fellow men. All the crap that a man has dealt you isn't your fault, but let me add that **you do have some responsibility.** See, it's not your fault that the majority of youth dropping out of high school are males, **but let me say that you do have some part in it.** You get upset that when you go off to college and the ratio of women to men is higher in every aspect. This is not your fault ladies, **but you do have some part in it!**

NOTE TO SELF: Sometimes it takes a queen to make a man recognize he is a king, especially if he was never privileged to be raised by one. What about the young man in college surrounded by intelligent women but has poor studying habits? He wants to ask for help, but the young lady thinks he is just trying to get in her pants not knowing that he is the first to go to college but ranked last to graduate. **Not your fault, but you may have some part in this.**

It's amazing to me that you may know of a woman who could be getting mentally, physically, and spiritually abused, yet you do nothing. It may not be your fault little lady, **but you do have some part in it.** You have probably heard of the woman who is always at the club in a man's face faithfully, yet she can't even get up in the morning to smile at her own beauty. Not your fault you say, **but I still believe you have some part in it.**

Of course, you know the mother who can't feed her child because the child's father took everything she had. Once again, **it's not your fault, but you do have some part in it.** You attend church or a certain spiritual home where the majority of the congregation is comprised of women, and the men that should be there are outside running around with no real morals. You shake your head in disgust saying that it isn't your fault, but my dear lady, **you do have some part in this.**

You hear about the woman who met this man one day, and she allows him to come to her home that same night. He sits on "HER" couch, eats "HER" food, watches "HER" television, and yet, he doesn't pay any of her bills. She allows him to complain about where she stays, but she owns her house, and he is still looking for a place to rent. It's not your fault that she allows this, but you may know her personally, so I say **you have some part in it.**

He runs this smooth talk on her about how beautiful she is and why he needs her. **"HE DECIDES"** that he wants to take her upstairs. So, she allows him to lead her upstairs to **"HER"** room and allows this **"STRANGER"** to lay **"HER BODY"** on **"HER BED."**

Now, let me pause this story line because two words were not stated and defined. One of these words is **"OWNERSHIP."** How can someone tell you what to do with your body if you own it? The second term is **"RELATIONSHIP."** Relationship means to relate. Do you think she has already made a connection before they decided to have relations? So, if they don't even relate, how is it that she is allowing him to exercise his leadership traits, or should I say, **"LEAD"** her **"SHIP"** to a location that could ruin her life? He hasn't done anything for her, but she is about to lower her values by opening her legs. Read these words very carefully my dear lady before you start making crazy decisions. No matter how old you are, the color of your skin, how much money you have, how you were raised, your past history with men, who your friends are, and what type of degree you hold...

If a man doesn't sweat for you,
don't let him sweat on you

What You Expect

Sometimes, the road gets tough. Some people choose to walk it alone while others seek refuge in the arms of strangers. Some tend to give up while others just walk forward while the tears fall to the ground. The travel may seem like an endless road. It may feel as though you are on the wrong path. Not too many people are speaking to you. Not too many people are around you. Not too many people are cheering you on. You watched some women walking back to where you once were. You walk past some who sit on the side of the road hoping that a car pulls up with an extra seat. The things you see while on your road can make you scared to go farther. It can make you want to give up. It can make you want to give up on life. It has the capacity to make you believe it's permissible to lower your standards. What do you expect when you take the road less traveled? It wasn't made for everyone - just the ones that have self-belief when everyone else believes in the opinions of others.

It's Called Love

I define love as the source of God. A person who has true love can be the Garden of Eden for another. Love allows you to not be judgmental of a person regardless of how many times he or she has tasted the forbidden fruit. Love is hard yet easy. It is confusing yet exciting. It is sweet and at times sour. Love can open doors for you, but sometimes too much love can shut them. Love has no form; it only has a source which is God. If you want to love a person with all your heart, you must first love the God in them. This is the only way you can "listen" and "understand" who they are. You will then see why they were made [perfectly] for you with these imperfections in an imperfect world.... LOVE.

The Reflection of Your Light

In the beginning of each year, some people make plans together, laugh together, start a family together, have a child together, work together, pray together, make love for the first time together, and some finally realize that it is best not to be together. God may even play a role by taking away some of the people we thought would be with us because he wanted them to be together.

You can learn so much but yet know so little. Did you know that people can disgrace you with the same mouth they praised you? Did you know that no one can live for you? Did you know that what we plan will always be shifted because God is in control?

Each year that we complete, we reflect more and more because memories preserve what will always change. And what will change are people, places, relationships, trends, cultures, and all the things that we, as human beings, become attached to and love. Reflecting helps us see where the shifts in our lives started, where the love began and ended, where we made the mistake, where we were most happy, where we were in the prime of our lives, and when we decided to take the chance that changed our lives forever.

As you embark on the next ten years of your life, embrace all that you hear and see. Embrace the beauty on the faces of those who will come and go out of your life, the melodies of life that will be heard, the vibration of God's heart as you lay on the chest of the one who loves you, the colors of dreams you will see when you can't sleep, and the invisible rainbow that can only be felt with conversations of happiness.

Words are powerful so use them carefully because they are the colors that will assist you in completing your masterpiece (your life).

Takes Time To Be Good Wine

Never rush into relationships or situations without taking the time to create "I can't wait until next time we meet" moments. I love having conversations with a woman who looks beautiful, holds great conversation, flirts, talks slick (I just love that), and can hold something back until the next time we meet. There's no need to rush. You have to be like wine, baby girl. The older the wine, the better it tastes. It takes time to become valuable. You have to hold back some things if you want the longevity of other things. I won't steer you wrong. Enjoy the chase. Enjoy the conversations. Enjoy the flirting and slick comments. Enjoy the wine....

Overdosing in Paris

Don't overdose on what [type] of woman you should be. Just [be] a woman. There are so many females who claim various types of labels as women but aren't built to fulfill the duties. The way you dress, how you speak, how you raise your kids, how you treat your friends, how you treat your man, the type of men you give time to, what you believe, and your lifestyle will define the type of woman you are.

No need to overdose on the things that don't matter. Just focus on being and loving you.

Make Sure Your Stilettos Are Stable

A blessed life is a life of stability. Your life is unstable when you can't keep a job, friends, money, female relationships, house, or things of the like. When you are blessed in life, you receive things that nobody else sees. Your blessings become so grand that you don't even know how to embrace them.

A woman that walks right in her stilettos knows she's blessed. Her life is blessed because she can live off her own fruits and nobody else's. She may break a heel once in a while, but she won't complain. She has the resources to fix it. She has a mind that thinks like a queen. She says, "I'm blessed, and I know that things like this happen in life. I have more than enough. I have had many great shoes in my life, and as long as I stay humble, I won't have to worry about one heel."

Are you stable? If not, change your shoe game and get your walk right.

He Chooses But You Accept

A man is the foundation that the family stands on. The woman and child stand on his shoulders. If the man of the family leaves, the woman and child will be measured by how tall he stood. Do you understand this? If the man [you] accepted in your life is weak, you must understand that your foundation will be weak (unless you're dealing with this right now). As a woman, you must make it a [standard] to become involved only with men who stand tall. It may be cute when you were young and watched as boys claimed they were men. But when you arrive at a certain age, such talk is no longer relevant. Actions become louder than words.

Take time with who you accept in your life. Men love the chase (I damn sure do), and great men have great stamina.

Boss Talk

Now, understand this.....

No woman of GREAT stature had it easy. She was not given a silver spoon next to her plate when it was time to eat. She knew what she was up against when she made the decision to be GREAT. Of course, it will be hard. Of course, you will run out of wind. Of course, you will fall. Of course, you will get back up. Of course, you will have to question if the support system of yesterday will be strong enough for the weight you will have to carry in the future. No woman of GREAT stature had it easy.

If you have too much on your plate right now, go on a diet. Eat only what is most important and then have the rest as leftovers for tomorrow. Preserve your figure! Preserve your health. Preserve your sanity.

No one will ever know what Superheroes endure after they have saved the planet, inspired a life, protected a family, or used their own life to help humanity. But I do. I know what you deal with, what keeps you up at night, and what has you second guessing sometimes.
But let me tell you something right now... you can do this.

You will do this because you were made for this.

Boyfriend vs. Husband

I really don't care if you are claiming to have a boyfriend or husband. If you are reading this book right now, then I'm your man. Period! But if this relationship doesn't work out, it's okay. At least I know that I gave you a new walk (wink).

When it comes to relationships, there has to be some lines drawn to understand the differences between them. I always have discussions with friends about the difference between boyfriends and husbands. There are several women who seem to never have good luck with men and relationships. The following are some things to consider.

There are many women who treat their boyfriends like husbands. These particular women give their man everything (for what reason I just don't know). When you ask them what they have saved for their future husbands, they won't have a clue what you're talking about.

Boyfriends aren't supposed to get everything, just as girlfriends aren't supposed to get everything. When a person is your boyfriend, there has to be something that he can't touch until he decides to make the full commitment. This principle applies for the girlfriend as well. Some women hold off on sex, children, and even moving in together. This is necessary because there has to be something that your significant other should experience that no other person you dated has already experienced.

Wouldn't you be pissed off if you got married and he took you to a fancy restaurant that he also previously took every one of his ex-girlfriends? Marriage is a level higher than boyfriend/girlfriend. It shows full commitment. It shows deeper maturity and respect. There are certain things that you will share or do that no other person has experienced.

Think about a person who dates and then finds a person with whom he or she wants to be in a committed relationship. Have you ever noticed how the person changes when in a relationship? How about when he or she is in love? There is a glow about that person. Why is this? It's because the person is experiencing something that others never have had a chance to see before. And you wonder why the ex-partners are stalking....

Be cautious not to give up EVERYTHING. It will be quite suspect if I was to ask you what will be the benefit of marrying you, and you respond, "Let me think about it."

Alpha Man

Have you ever had an ALPHA man? I'm not talking the fraternity brother; I'm talking about the man that will have you thinking twice about your choices in life. After I give you these lessons, some of you may have to leave the man you are with. Hey, if you know better, you will do better.

An ALPHA man is one who protects and provides for his woman. He makes it a habit to assist her in her balance with mind, body, and soul. He wants to see her win and climb to the top of her mountain. He doesn't care about the designer labels; he just wants to make sure she has something to wear every day. He makes sure she has eaten. He prays for her every day. He makes sure that before she walks out into the world, she is well-prepared. He makes sure she has a roof over her head. And if the roof has a leak, he does everything in his power to make sure it's patched correctly. He ensures she has her bills paid and that her stress level is low.

It's very interesting to watch a woman who deals with a man who isn't an ALPHA man. She comes out of the house looking like she has no pride in her appearance. Her stress levels are through the roof. Her thoughts are always negative because of the environment with which she is dealing. In no way should a man allow his woman out of the house looking like a werewolf! I would be pissed off! If you have a man, you must understand that you are an extension of him (and vice versa).

If a good woman deals with a man who's spirit isn't right, her life will become unbalanced. She is the earth, and he is the sun. If his light is dull and far in the distance, she will feel winter during her summer season. Never be this woman. If you are this woman at the moment, change the season now. Shift to a new galaxy and make note to bask in the sunlight of a man that shines bright for an earth such as you.

Never Go Unnoticed in the World

Relationships are important. When you form a bond with an individual or decide to get married, this means you both made a promise to NEVER let both of your lives go unnoticed in the world. We all need witnesses for our lives which is why relationships are important in the world.

In the Meantime

"In the meantime" is a term that you should love to say to yourself. When you feel as though you can't find that man to call your own, you should stop looking and have an "in the meantime" moment. So now, when you stop looking, you can spend time focusing on yourself "in the meantime." When you are feeling like stress is taking over your mind and body, hit the spa "in the meantime."

Sometimes, individuals forget that it's the "in the meantime" moments that you upgrade yourself, view your mistakes, and have great conversations with people you never thought could hold one. That is why you should always try to have an empty space called... "IN THE MEANTIME."

Blessing: Even when others can't value their time, make sure to let others know what YOUR time means to you.

Piano Keys

At one point, the day may appear black and white, but you can play musical notes in your day by doing positive deeds. Some people will give you the feeling of darkness while others give you the view of white positive light. Play on both colors to give yourself a Mozart rhapsody in your walk. Piano keys in your life are the talks that you have with people that make you think of your favorite song. The keys are the smiles that you give to people that make their heart skip a beat. It is the prayers that are answered along with an extra note (blessing). Even though everyone has piano keys, it doesn't mean that everyone knows how to play them.

Blessing: May your day be filled with music of joy, melodies of hope, and beats of passion.

Getting the Right Advice

Getting the right advice is something for which you must always aim. As humans, we tend to ask best friends and close family members for advice, but are you realizing who they are? If someone is having consistent downfalls in his or her own relationships, how can he or she help you? Why would you want their advice unless you want an unhealthy relationship? Some people accept their girl's opinion as the golden rule, but sometimes the advice isn't valuable at all. What if she is having an ongoing financial crisis? What can she give you for advice except telling you to not follow what she is doing? Be careful who you get advice from because although they may mean well, it can still destroy you.

Always make sure that the people you get advice from have been through the experience and/or received some sound insight. Make sure people have something to substantiate their advice they provide you as well. How can someone tell you how to cook a full course meal when they always eat out? Practice makes perfect, and if they don't practice what they preach, then they can't teach a perfect lesson.

Keep advisors around you so that you won't put your life in ruins. As a woman, you must know where you stand and what you must do to keep your family together as well as yourself.

Blessings: May you stand firm with pearls around your neck, a crown of wisdom around your head, and a circle of advisors around your life.

Lesson Learned

It's alright to say that you messed up, but it should be a lesson learned. It's okay to say that you gave the wrong person more trust than they should have warranted, but it was a lesson learned. If you are more than what you went through yesterday, it was a lesson learned. It must have been a great one because you never returned to that lesson. I must say I am proud of you because so many females are still trying to learn the lesson you have already received.

Never think that lessons are only for a moment. As long as you live, you will receive lessons from life in which you are tested before the lesson. However, once you receive and pass the test, it goes on your report card which is your history and experience.

If you are experiencing a test right now, just know that it will be over as soon as you learn the lesson. Some tests are longer or shorter than others. But until you learn the lesson, you will be stuck with the test. Take your time and evaluate everything that is going on in your life... if it isn't worth the study, remove it and move on to the next subject.

Blessing: May the lessons learned help develop you into a beautiful woman and show all the wonders of the world in your eyes.

The True Super Woman

A super woman is the woman who takes care of the kids that the father didn't want to assist with. The true super woman is the female who is low on funds but high in hopes! She is the one who goes out on the edge for her man when he is down just so she can help bring him up. She is the one who cares for her brothers and sisters because her mother can't do it by herself.

The true super woman is the "go-getter," the everyday woman, and the college graduate at 40 years of age with a full time job with kids. She is the real hero! She is also the mother who lost her son in war but still manages to smile every day.

You are appreciated even when you may think you are not. Through all the issues in the world, you are still walking tall, smiling bright, and giving love more than Valentine's Day. Keep moving, keep shaking, and keep flying.

Blessing: May the life you live be an example to another female of the true definition of heroism.

Tired of Being Sick and Tired

See, when you realize it's time to leave, it means that you have grown up. When you are tired of losing, being put last, and receiving negative talk, it's time to change. Why must you put yourself through the pain and agony of being tired of being sick and tired? When will you realize that you only have one life and it should not be spent with hurt, pain, sadness, and mediocrity?

In this day and age, you need to "HAVE" solitude. You need to "HAVE" peace of mind and good health. We understand that relationships are something that we want but not if they are going to bring us down. If the relationship you are in (this goes for friendships too) makes you tired and sick, then why bother? Healthy relationships experience their share of ups and downs but not regularly.

Why be stuck at a job that drains you and where you aren't happy? What makes you think that you can't lock down another position with your intelligence, experience, and character? Stop being sick and tired! Go be happy and excited about everything with which you are involved.

Leave those negative comments for the birds! Let someone who doesn't care enjoy the sorrow. You must get yourself fed up to the point where you understand this statement... enough is enough!

Blessing: May your days be long so you can enjoy life with extended love and happiness.

Keep Walking

Let's start by saying, "Keep walking, and don't look back." When you feel that he will stop hitting you, stay strong and keep walking past that thought. When they say you can't get that house, just smile and keep walking to the bank. When they say you won't be a great mother, just hold your head up and keep walking to the baby isle. When they say you can't get that degree, just state a quote from a great leader and walk to your next class. When they are in doubt, just walk with confidence.

Keep yourself in great shape by walking forward. So many females stand still because they let their past and dream killers keep them from walking forward. You are strong in your strut, fierce on your cat walk of life, and will not break a heel when you full turn. When they say stop walking, smile and start running. When they say stop running, slow down, look back in the rear view mirror and pull off in your car.

Blessing: Walk in your greatness and always maintain your patience.

The Drama Woman

We all know the drama woman or as some like to call her...The Drama Queen. This is the woman that seeks to dismantle happy homes because she isn't happy on her own. This is the woman who spreads other people's problems but can't handle her own. This is for the people who get tired of hearing the female that seems to be in everyone's business yet can't invest in her own. This is for the women who tried to be nice, but the drama queen took advantage and put their husband/boyfriend issues on the line. I think this is the time to watch your back because when you think your winning, you have already lost.

It's amazing how these women act with so much drama. They make you feel like you are in a Daytime TV Soap series. I know you ask yourself time and time again, "How can drama queens be this old and still act childish?"

As you nod your head in agreement, what about when you are at work? There always seems to be that one particular female that everyone knows is a trouble maker. If she is a teacher, she is always in that teachers' lounge waiting on her prey. If she is in a corporate office, she is doing the same in the lunch or copy room. You will always have people like this, and you must recognize them so you can avoid their negative behavior. What good will you gain from them? The answer is nothing but a headache and a temper once you discover she has been spreading your information.

Blessing: May you recognize fools and be wise to avoid them because as long as you hang around fools, the better your chance will be of becoming one.

Why Set Low Standards

Standards come from those who have specific goals that they would love to accomplish. They keep an individual on track so that they don't lose sight of their goals. One must never compare his or her goals to those of another person because what you want may not be what they desire. When you look at what you want out of life, you can't be frugal with your standards. Set them high yet attainable. What type of people do you want to socialize with? What type of a boyfriend or husband do you want to deal with? What are the basic credentials? What type of mentor, staff, team, study group, or business partners do you want to associate with?

Understand that realistically, people will not meet every standard that you have for them whether it is high or low. But there should be specific things for which you will not lower your standards. Why should you set low standards? Don't you know men like a chase? Did you know that we find it enjoyable when we have to work for we want? It's the only way someone can really appreciate what they receive. When you give something away easily without work, it will lose value quicker than a second in time.

So I ask you, why set low standards for yourself and the things you want? Didn't Maya Angelou say you are a phenomenal woman... phenomenally? Therefore, set phenomenal goals with personal standards... phenomenally.

Blessing: Keep your standards strong so that you always keep a solid foundation.

Relationships

Relationships are defined differently to each person you meet. Yet, some individuals fail to give you a solid explanation why in this day and age people fall out of relationships quickly. When I say the term "relationship," I am not just referring to boyfriend and girlfriend. I am also talking about family, friends, business, and spiritual relationships that seem to fall short.

It seems people don't understand that they don't relate to another individual as time progresses. Having a relationship means to relate. So I must ask you... do you relate to each person you call a friend and family member? If the answer is no, then why do you deal with him or her? Don't you know that this can hold you back? If an individual doesn't RELATE to you, why allow him or her on your SHIP to view the scenery?

We all possess the quality of leadership in our lives, but again, most people don't look at the term deeply enough. Leadership is more of a personal question asking, "Who leads your ship?" Is it the wrong people who think they relate to you? Are they giving you information that isn't of assistance but rather destroys you? Or are you the person directing your ship? Let people around you know that you are confident with where you stand and that you understand where you are going. Also, let those around you know that if they are not in tune with their own self, there is no basis for the two of you to have a healthy relationship together.

Blessing: May you always fly with hawks and never have time to converse with chickens because they can't fly.

Yesterday

Waiting yesterday for today may have been a long moment for you. However, you are here strong and well-prepared for tomorrow. The pain you endured is over, and today you can cry with joy instead of pain. There is no need to hide the beautiful thoughts of who you are and who you plan to be. What a day it was yesterday, but it is even more beautiful today because the storm is over!

Always believe in the faith you had yesterday today because today will be yesterday tomorrow. Got that? Games will be played today, but tomorrow someone will end up losing while the other person wins. Rather than playing games, keep it real so you don't have to tell a story about losing something yesterday because of the games you played today.

Blessing: Believe in yourself today because tomorrow will bring you blessings greater than most due to the faith you planted today.

Mother 2 Be

A life is something so unique, deep in emotions, and a new vessel that carries a piece of God within. You are about to experience motherhood. Some have motherhood as a goal in life while others wish they could have the opportunity. So I say to you with as much love behind it as possible... Congratulations! May you have so many blessings that come your way that you pray for expansion of your territory just so you have more than enough room to receive them.

But I ask you to do me a favor, and that is to be the best mother possible. Your child may hold the cure to an illness, be the next leader of your country, or be the answer to your personal problems. Grow your child to be more than average because each life is special. Let him or her know that they have gifts and talents. Ensure they are strong in the areas where you are weak.

If the father isn't in the picture, make sure your child has a male role model. Finally, always let them know that a mother's love can never be replaced, even though they will already know because you decided to give them life.

Blessing: May your child be a blessing.

Luggage in a New Relationship

We all have issues in relationships. However, we must not carry these issues into new relationships. Instead, we must find a way to solve problems that we have with someone as well as those with which we have with ourselves. Do not to judge a person because of the hurt another person has previously caused you. I suggest you learn and grow from the past issue, but don't try to solve it in the new relationship. The new person didn't cause you hurt, pain, or anger. So why dump scraps on a plate when you haven't even prepared dinner yet?

You may have heard of not bringing old luggage to a new vacation. This means don't bring your issues to your new relationship (friendly or romantic). Before becoming involved in a new relationship, make sure you have remediated the issues that you were having personally and with others. If you don't, you may cause an unnecessary pile up of problems.

So, make sure you unpack your winter clothes in order to pack your spring clothing. It will be difficult trying to manage everything, especially when you want to bring four seasons of issues to your vacation (individual).

Blessing: The less you bring, the more room you have to pack for new experiences.

Revolving Door

I had the opportunity to talk to a few powerful, educated, and successful women as I decided to write this book. As they were talking to me, I noticed they really wanted to communicate what some of the females who may read this book should know. To see one woman express her experiences and what she learned made me understand certain strengths that a strong woman possesses.

One piece of advice shared with me was to never let your home be a revolving door. I have a god-daughter now, and I may have a daughter of my own in the future. I want the best advice to go to my children so they won't fall through the cracks of life.

Again, do not let your home be a revolving door. Why should every man have the privilege to be in your home, eat the food that you prepared, sleep in your bed, or even meet your children? Your life will end in ruins with all those "short-term" relationships! What will you do when your children, who will also start a relationship with this individual, ask why he has suddenly left? Your son and daughter will now believe that they have ten uncles, yet you have no real brothers.

A revolving door in your life will drain your energy, and it scares the children as they grow and begin to view the world in which they live. The lesson they will have learned when watching how you lived will now be passed along to their children. Ultimately, the downward cycle continues that could have been broken by you.

Blessing: May you have doors in your life that open to longevity and prosperity but are locked to protect from thieves.

Self Esteem

The *New American Dictionary* defines "esteem" as **to set a high value on**. Then, the second definition states **to rate**. However, the third and final definition is **respect**. As a young man, I see several females, both young and older, who suffer from low self-esteem. It may be because there was no strong role model in their home during their upbringing. Likewise, it may be because there wasn't a father figure who could confirm that the lessons of her mother or teacher were correct. Or maybe no one was listening when she cried rape, abuse, or pain.

As a responsible, educated, and savvy lady, it is your responsibility to be of great esteem. There are so many females from every background who need to see you walk with self-esteem as a crown on your head. The strength of your words of advice should match the strength of your walk. As a female, don't talk if a man sees you as walking backwards.

If you are the female who struggles with self-esteem, understand that you must aim high. Don't wait for a man to buy you a drink; buy one yourself because you can hold your own. Don't be in a man's face when you can't even look at your own in the mirror. You must be empowered to go high.

The past is the past! We cannot change our history, but we can use today to ensure we do not experience the past in the future. Take time to build your character by talking to individuals who are successful and have great character, personality, and lifestyle.

Blessing: Let go with dignity, let go with respect gained, let go with strength, and let go with self–esteem

Difference Between Two Children

This information is for those who have an opinion about other people's kids. There is a difference between a child that is rough and one who is treated rough. The child that is rough is hard-headed and always getting into things even when he or she was told otherwise. The rough child is hard on the heart and needs attention to determine his or her problem. Likewise, the child is from parents who don't have control over him or her. Specifically, they allow the child to talk back, and when the child is disrespectful, the parents think it's cute. They don't realize that the child is making things difficult for you and the people who come in contact with their "Dennis the Menace."

The child that is treated rough can sometimes be mistaken by the rough child because he or she looks rough. He or she can be full of smiles with disheveled hair or hair that is never done. They are great students but don't have school supplies. They are the ones who are always hungry and have a tendency to ask for something to eat. You must see the difference. They may have a strong father but no mother figure, and it makes them rough on females with their words.

Knowing the difference between these types of children allows you to keep a watchful eye for your own kids. It should be your goal to keep your children out of both of these boxes by always paying attention to their needs and wants. Understand what they are expressing and to whom they are expressing themselves. Know the difference for your child or children.

Blessing: Love your child as much as possible.

Pump Your Brakes Little Lady

We are not to far off in age, but I feel compelled to let you know that we can relate on many issues. So with that, I must say we have so much to live for before we make certain decisions. Before you take that sip of the alcohol, consider the consequences. Before you decide to open your legs, make sure he is really there for you if the condom breaks. Ensure before you leave school that you have real support just in case the job decides to lay you off. Pump your brakes before it becomes too late. Before you decide to use that needle, pop that pill, or lose your virginity tonight, ensure that you are prepared for the outcome. One pill can destroy your precious life. Likewise, that jewel between your legs may be considered of no value when he gets up and tells his boys.

Pump your brakes! Before he runs game, make sure you know that you may lose if you decide to join in as a player. Pump your brakes and visit the doctor because what you may not know can shorten your life or that of your future child you are holding in your womb. There will always be parties, and there will always be a man who will try to impress you. There will always be another chance to mess up your life, but there may not be another chance to leave the darkness and enjoy life's light.

Pump your brakes and enjoy life! Pump your brakes to negative talk and people! Pump your brakes on the road that leads to nowhere, but hit the gas to turn around and proceed in the right direction.

Blessing: May your life change for the good and for the negative because of immature peer pressure.

Homeless Woman

When you are feeling down, you must pray for strength. When you receive strength, take productive actions to remove yourself from the situation. Never think that you are at the end of the road. As long as you live, you still have a road of life to travel. Many people believe their life is over when they experience a mid-life crisis, a painful experience, or a loss of what they considered their most prized possession. Don't you know that you have to remove some little things in your life to make room for something great?

There is nothing wrong with becoming emotional when the bad experience first occurs. But when you realize that it has happened, accept that there is nothing more you can do and move on. I know what it feels like to lose everything; I have seen a woman who struggled with four boys because she lost the only man she loved. If you are struggling, let it be a beautiful struggle in which you have grown for the better.

You can make it! You can do this! You may have lost your house, but you can have a mansion in the hills. You may have lost your job, but you can obtain your degree and start over with a new career. Try it! Show the world why you are strong, and no matter the lemons that life gives you, know that you can make lemonade by turning something sour into something sweet. Drink it right in its face!

You have nowhere to go now **EXCEPT UP!**

Blessing: Your location isn't your destination.

No Means No

I am going to flip this statement because we hear it so much in reference to males. However, the same statement applies for women as well. **When you are romantically involved with a man, you may have aspirations, goals, dreams, or ideas for weddings, but that may be only your desires.**

Did I lose you yet? See, there are some females that hear a man say, "I don't like you" or "I am really not interested." He may even get to the point where he constantly hangs up on you (sorry, I mean "her"). But this female tends to still pursue him like he is the man for her when he was very clear to her that he did not feel the same.

See, when you know that you have value and something to bring to the table, you won't have to beg. You won't have to sit by the phone for the entire weekend to wait on his call. These are the actions that tend to happen when you are quick to assume that he is truly interested in you, especially when he hasn't even said so.

If he says no, then **No means No.**

"No, I really don't think we are making progress."

"No, I am not feeling you."

"No, I don't want to meet your parents."

"No, I didn't make 10 year plans for us (how many weeks have we been dating?)"

"No, I am already dating someone."

"No, I don't think it's cool to have sex on this one night. I don't even know you."

So, if you still don't understand this statement of "No Means No," then return and re-read the section on self-esteem.

Heaven

In vows and promises lies Heaven. In finished business and healthy conversation, Heaven speaks and rewards. As you grow through a world of fame and change, Heaven shines brighter with stability. At times, there will be people who you meet who you believe are angels, but you start second guessing yourself. Stick to your first choice because if you were smiling when speaking to them, you were in Heaven. In Heaven, angels are met, goals are achieved, promises are kept, problems are solved, information makes sense, and love is overflowing.

In Heaven, God shows off. He reveals the expansion of your territory so that you can enjoy all of your blessings. Heaven becomes your cat walk, and it shows off all the blessings with which GOD has dressed you. It is here that smiles are of gratitude, salute, passion, and happiness for you. Heaven is a goal we try to reach each and every day. It is the location of cloud nine. It is where harps are played and your heart begins to dance. It is here that truth tells you the truth. It is where you are able to see the reflections of what you put out into the world days before. So if you were in Heaven yesterday and put out goodness there, then what makes you think that you are not in Heaven today reaping what you sowed yesterday?

Blessing: That is what you are... a blessing.

Beating the Pink Slip

I dedicate this to the female who was given the pink slip from life. Never believe that this pink slip is the symbol of your discontinuation of life. You are a strong, dynamic, and courageous female. Remember in our "Lessons Learned" where I stated, **"Life is the only teacher that gives you the test before the lesson."**

I have met many females who were given the pink slip, and I watched them automatically destroy it soon after it was issued to them. They didn't believe that their service in the career world of life was not needed. They knew that they were needed and that there were other job positions that they could fulfill!

There are many bosses in the career world of life. Some of them like to break down the female (if the female allows them to). **Don't let them break you down** to where it causes them to say you are doing a poor job and issues you a pink slip. I have heard stories of bosses who have issued or "tried" to issue these pink slips but could not do it.

That's because these particular women stood up to these pink slip bosses by saying, "I deserve to be here in this position. I deserve to be strong while doing this job in life! And if you feel that issuing me a pink slip is going to weaken me, you have another thing coming, honey."
So I say this to you as a representative of the brother, the friend, the boyfriend, the son, the husband, the grandfather, the uncle, and god-parent... be strong in your fight! Be courageous in your fight! Be faithful in

your fight! Each day is a battle, and you may feel like you lose some of those battles, but you can and will win the war!

I pray for you my fair lady! And if I never get a chance to meet you, just know that I truly LOVE YOU!

Blessing: To be one of the many antidotes for the Cure for Cancer.

126 Pocketbook Quotes
by RahGor

Shhhh......
Just let me talk and touch.
I promise you'll like it.

"When I was young, I dated Failure, but I dumped her for Victory; then, I noticed that victory wasn't as sexy as Success, so I left victory for her. Now, I met a new love and her name is History. Years from now, she will talk about my relationships and all the things we've done together. But I have to enjoy her now, so I nicknamed her Present because of all the gifts she is helping me see in my life."

"Don't lose yourself while trying to find yourself."

"Pursue happiness and not money."

"As human beings, we are **all** supposed to **evolve**. Staying the same **shows** lack of **growth**."

"You have to **transform** your world from within to **create** the world you want to see."

"Know success not according to the standards of the world but according to the standards that you set for yourself."

"It's about **enjoying** the process, so if you enjoy the journey, the goal isn't as **important** as the process; especially when you understand. Why wait to feel joy after the goal is **accomplished?** Be **happy** along the way."

"When you **begin** to use your inner gift to its highest potential, **God** will make you **known**."

"If you have something in your life or home that is broken, either you fix it or throw it out. You do this because everything speaks in volumes to your spirit. Why would you allow brokenness to be the spokes-person for your life? Allowing broken things to be in your home or life confirms you have no comfort zone. One must always find ways to fix or throw out the things that try to move into the comfort zone."

"There will **always** be someone who will hate that you have **favor** over your life. So what else is new?"

"Focus on the **process** because you **already** know the goal."

"Inventory check yourself everyday."

"Don't believe that everyone will be there for you when needed."

"Just because they go to school with you doesn't mean they know everything you're going through."

"Always **remember** that money helps **invest** in your passion; money is a **tool**, not a goal."

"Keep your mind on valuable and worthy things. This will eventually manifest into reality."

"What if" is negative. That's thinking negative on things that are not even in the present."

"Love yourself to the point that you don't need anybody to confirm you look good or you're doing a good job."

"You have to ACCEPT that life is good!"

"The universe likes speed. Don't delay. Don't second **guess**. Don't doubt. When **opportunity** is there, when the impulse is there, when the **intuitive** nudge from within is there, **ACT!** That's your job! And that's all you have to do!"

"Your aim could be **GREAT** but you may have to change your target."

"Learn to get off the boat with haters and doubters so you can walk on water."

"Life is **simple**. The people you **choose** to be around and the **situations** you put **yourself** in, makes it complicated."

"Expand your **consciousness** and you will shift the world."

"We were **perfectly** made imperfect to **fulfill** our purpose perfectly in a world that focuses on our **imperfections.**"

"Every **moment** you have a choice; but you must remember you have **unlimited** choices. Every **moment** is a moment to be amazing and **powerful**."

"Don't be fooled; just because some women have a fancy title doesn't mean they fulfill the duties that come with it."

"What you **learn** and **believe** will be cross-examined by life's experiences."

"The higher you go, the harder the test. Each test you pass, the greater the reward."

"If HE helped you pay the rent, then he will help you pay for the mortgage. If HE helped you pay for the bus pass, he will help you pay the car note."

"Every gift isn't for the **current** season."

"The things you want the most are the hardest to work for."

"God knows what you want; that's why certain prayers won't get answered."

"You don't have to see it to speak it."

"Your words can put you into bondage or take you out of it."

"Always **remember** that your words are containers like drinking glasses. You **must always** check yourself by saying, "What are my words **containing**? Positive or negative energy? Always be **aware** of what you are **serving** the people in your life."

"Stay **humble** because you never know when you will fumble."

"You must stand out to fit in."

"Some men you may come in contact with may have a great body but a dying soul."

"Some females dress how they think while others need to think about how they dress."

"At times like this, you will have to think backwards to move forward. Conversation before sex. Marriage before kids. Thinking before speaking. Asking before assuming. Loving rather than hating."

"Don't be scared to be **different** because you just might make a difference."

"You know what's sexy.... your power, **influence,** and answers to the problems. To know that you are the key to **solving** some of the problems in life is **amazing** to me. The way you can **calm** a child who is **frustrated while** showing off your beauty with little effort is just **sexy** to me...."

"You can be hurt then leave, or you can leave so you won't be hurt."

"Find the good in goodbye."

"Treasure is something that's stored. Your treasure chest is your mouth and as soon as you open it, you reveal the true treasure of your heart."

"Our lives are like a river; you can't step into the same river twice or experience this life more than once because just like currents in the river, they are always changing."

"You can never **win** when you continue to look back at the past and **remain** in that **emotional** state. The best is not yet to come if you are **stuck** in the past."

"If you are not at **peace** with yourself, then you can't be at peace with **others.**"

"Sometimes you have let go to hold on."

"The wounds that hurt the most are the ones you can't see with the human eye. The wounds that can have you handicapped in the future are the ones you never let heal in the past."

"What comes easy will leave fast; those things that you work hard on will last a lifetime."

"Be memorable."

"[Heels] can heal, and the right [clutch] can show others you have a grip on your life."

"If you want to **dress** for your man, wear **nothing**."

"If you can't dress your **mind** with great **thoughts**, it doesn't matter what type of label you wear on your body."

"The most **beautiful** make-up a woman can wear is her **character.**"

"Never treat your **life** like a piece of **clothing** on the **clearance** rack. You are custom made."

"There is a **difference** between a woman that can walk into a room and command **attention** by her presence and a woman that **walks** into a room **screaming** for attention by what she wears."

"Life is one big **rollercoaster.** Some **days** you will be going up and some days you will be going down. No matter which **direction** you are currently going in, just enjoy the ride."

"Sometimes, the way you receive a hug can feel better than a kiss. Sometimes the way you receive a kiss can feel better than a hug."

"Just because a person doesn't show off his or her wings doesn't mean he or she is not an angel."

"Deal with your own issues before subscribing to someone else's."

"A good stroke can always help the ego when you need confidence."

"Good girls follow **everything** by the book and **rarely** meet the author. It's okay to break the rules **every** now and then to **experience** something or someone different."

"Judge a man by his **principles** to **determine** if the **partnership** will be invincible."

"You will **never** know what it's like to be on the other side until you **cross** the line."

"I learned that you can't make permanent decisions with temporary information."

"The **break up** was probably **needed** so you could move up."

"You can't be the queen bee if you allow everyone into your beehive."

"Old friends and **partners** may throw rocks but it's nothing like **seeing yourself** rise when you use them as stepping stones."

"Some **people** say they want to know the real you. And when the real you is **revealed,** some will eventually **runaway.** So **cherish** the ones who keep it real with you. These are the ones who are **quick** to **check** you but also the ones who are quick to catch you."

"A man doesn't need to put his **woman** on a **pedestal.** If he is working out every day, he can **hold** her up."

"If you make love to your life every day, it will always put you in new positions."

"Never be scared to pave the way even if it means telling some people you love to move because they are in your way."

"No matter who **leaves** your side, you still have to **ride** and survive! The best life surfers are the ones **everyone** loves to watch from the **beach** as they keep their balance during the high tides. If I can keep my **balance,** I know you can too."

"LOVE yourself first because in this world people have a tendency to put you second."

"Some of you are **reaching** for something that you are already touching. And some of you are **searching** for someone you already have."

"Do you want to know what makes a great man? The answer is trial and error."

"We meet people at **different** times in our lives. Some we meet when we're not too **knowledgeable** about ourselves. Some we meet while we are going through personal **transformations**. And some we meet once we have a clear understanding of who we are. But no matter the stage we are currently on, everyone you meet is for a reason. God doesn't create things by **mistake**, he creates things on purpose for a **purpose**."

"In a **relationship**, real conversation and interaction is so **essential.** I love kissing my woman so much that her cheek forms a **dimple.** I think of it as leaving evidence that affection **enhances** beauty to the temple."

"There are people who are great for dating (short-term) but horrible for marriage (long-term). Then you have those who are built for marriage but horrible at dating (short-term relationship). Healthy conversations usually can help you with determining the role a person plays. Usually when asked about personal goals, family interaction, and the role of partnership, you can either see passion or distraction."

"Just because some of your friends and associates aren't where you are doesn't mean you have to dim your lights to make them feel better. It's your time to shine. Everyone will have their time, and if they don't use it, God will take it back and give it to someone who will. Never compromise your light to share in someone else's darkness."

"Don't waste your time walking an extra mile for someone who is going in the opposite direction."

"Change starts from within
not with him."

"You can let people in your life be whatever they want to be; just don't let them be your downfall."

"Sometimes you have to **subtract** some people from your **equation**. Because truth be told, you **plus** them doesn't **add** up to much. Which more than likely is the **problem**."

"Sex should be **exclusive**. Not everyone should enjoy the **experience** with you."

"Through sickness and health.... When your mate **tells** you he has **cancer**, when relationship storms come, when truth becomes lies and **when** lies become the truth, will you still stick it out? When he loses his job and you have to be the breadwinner for the **moment**, when outer beauty is no more and all you both are left with is **character,** are you really ready for a relationship? Just a moment of clarity."

"Love is more than a word. Making love is more than sex. Relationships are more than a title. Marriage is more than the wedding day. Communication is more than talking. Learn how to be and grow evenly yoked in a relationship so that your tissues won't be completed soaked."

"If you know it's not **good** news, why spread it? If you know negative energy lives there why visit? If you hate your **environment** so much why do you reside there? In an energy driven world, you must **understand** that positive and negative energy doesn't vanish; they just shift to where most people feed it or become the vessel for it."

"A man cannot leave a **better** legacy to the world than a well-**educated** family. And a man cannot make a better place for **himself** in the sun if he keeps taking refuge under the **family** tree."

"Today, don't **search** for the perfect lover; instead, create the perfect love. We all have something **inside** that needs to be given to the outside. Take time to **be still,** so you can feel what is stirring on the inside."

"I look at **flirtation** as letting a beautiful woman know she has my valuable **attention** without me having any disrespectful **intention**."

"Never forget the ones that **help** you shine because no **matter** how bright your light there are moments when you will need your **bulb** changed."

"You should **respect** a man who isn't afraid to chase the woman he wants because it will reveal the type of shape he's in."

"Chasing your **dream** will cause some friends to run out of breath. First, they stop running alongside you and then they stop calling you from a distance. So, due to the lack of training in the **relationship**, one loses his or her pace with life. But you cannot slow up because you have to keep running forward while **staying** focused on your mission."

"Be wise about what you share with those around you. Not everyone has your best interests at heart. Always think twice but speak once."

"Some people **think** they are progressing when they are only moving next door to a **nicer** apartment on the same **bad** street."

"Listen closely. Stop knocking what you hate and start supporting what you love. You give power and attention to what you don't like when you talk about it. Yet, you starve what you love when you don't give it all of your energy and attention."

"If you let anyone drink from your river, there may come a time when a good person may come around and look at your water as possibly being contaminated. They may also feel that you do not have enough clean water to satisfy their thirst in life. So don't let the wrong people contaminate your water. Preserve it so you can quench the right person's thirst."

"Keep your vision clear so you can stay on the driver's side of the car you want to steer."

"Keep a diverse set of **successful** people in your **circle**. Make sure they can sharpen your skills just as **much** as you are sharpening theirs."

"A second chance can sometimes look better than a first impression."

"I hate to see **when** people had it and then lose it. Makes you wonder what the **heck** people in their **circle** were telling them."

"You shouldn't settle for what isn't yours."

"Feeling right at home isn't the same as sitting at home."

"Nothing like having someone to hug for no reason."

"Love has no color."

"Always check EGO. If you use it incorrectly, you will watch
[E]verything [Go]."

"I was once told that **fake** friends are like shadows; they are always near you during your **brightest** moments but nowhere to be seen in your darkest moments."

"People always tend to believe they know what lies ahead."

"It's not the people I leave **behind** that hurts because **everyone** plays their part at certain times. What seem to hurt the most is the people I was **supposed** to reach but couldn't because I held on to certain ones I was supposed to **leave** behind."

"There isn't **anything** wrong with feeling and looking **sexy**."

"Diamonds are **created** by two elements – Darkness and Pressure."

"If he can't choose between you and the other woman, he already did."

"A man will **chase** and fight for what he believes he deserves."

"Observe how he **treats** his family."

"Men and women are not mind readers. If you don't say what's on your mind, don't expect someone to hear the words that were never said."

"You have two options with a man:
Whisper that you like it
or
Show him how you like it."

"The most **boring** authors are the ones who tell you to do **everything** by the book. Never take their advice."

"You will **never** know that you could do it until you **begin** to do it."

"A woman that **believes** there is a man that hasn't made any major mistake in his life is **crazy** and probably by herself. Always remember that a man that hasn't made any **mistakes** is make-believe (imagination can be so funny)."

"If it scares you and **excites** you at the same **time**, that's the path you should be walking."

"I know a few **good** girls that write in their **dairies** every night. It's too bad that they will never know how it feels to **write** about **riding** with the top down at night under the stars in the **fast** lane."

Vous êtes plus belle que les étoiles
www.RahGor.com

www.ingramcontent.com/pod-product-compliance
Lightning Source LLC
LaVergne TN
LVHW051558070426
835507LV00021B/2642